HAUNTED! EDINBURGH CASTLE

Gareth Stevens
Publishing

BY RYAN NAGELHOUT

Please visit our website, www.garethstevens.com. For a free color catalog of all our high-quality books, call toll free 1-800-542-2595 or fax 1-877-542-2596.

Library of Congress Cataloging-in-Publication Data

Nagelhout, Ryan.

Haunted! Edinburgh Castle / by Ryan Nagelhout.

    p. cm. — (History's most haunted)

Includes index.

ISBN 978-1-4339-9254-4 (pbk.)

ISBN 978-1-4339-9255-1 (6-pack)

ISBN 978-1-4339-9253-7 (library binding)

1. Edinburgh Castle (Edinburgh, Scotland)—Juvenile literature. 2. Castles—Scotland—Edinburgh—History—Juvenile literature. 3. Edinburgh (Scotland)—Buildings, structures, etc.—Juvenile literature 4. Ghosts—Juvenile literature. I. Nagelhout, Ryan. II. Title.

DA890.E4 N34 2014

133.1'29—dc23

First Edition

Published in 2014 by
Gareth Stevens Publishing
111 East 14th Street, Suite 349
New York, NY 10003

Copyright © 2014 Gareth Stevens Publishing

Designer: Nicholas Domiano
Editor: Kristen Rajczak

Photo credits: Cover, p. 1 jan kranendonk/Shutterstock.com; p. 4 cristapper/Shutterstock.com; p. 5 Photodisc/Thinkstock; p. 7 Postdlf/Wikimedia Commons; pp. 8, 16 iStockphoto/Thinkstock; p. 9 Kim Traynor/Wikimedia Commons; p. 11 Karl Borg/Flickr/Getty Images; p. 13 Leemage/Universal Image Group/Getty Images; p. 14 photo courtesy of WIkimedia Commons, James III, King of Scotland.png; p. 15 John Slezer/Wikimedia Commons; p. 17 photo courtesy of Matthew Wells/www.flickr.com/coastermadmatt; pp. 19, 21 Ad Meskens/Wikimedia Commons; p. 23 Morag Fleming/Shutterstock.com; p. 25 Tamara Kulikova/Shutterstock.com; p. 27 Anna Kucherova/Shutterstock.com; p. 29 godrick/Shutterstock.com.

Printed in the United States of America

CPSIA compliance information: Batch #CS13GS: For further information contact Gareth Stevens, New York, New York at 1-800-542-2595.

CONTENTS

Castle Rock 4

First Settlers 6

Back and Forth 8

Escape Gone Wrong 10

The Black Dinner 12

The Nor' Loch. 14

Crown Square 16

Lady of Glamis. 18

Greyfriars Bobby 20

Musical Ghosts. 22

The Experiment 26

Castle Rock Today 28

Glossary. 30

For More Information 31

Index 32

Words in the glossary appear in **bold** type the first time they are used in the text.

CASTLE ROCK

Sitting on what's left of an ancient **volcano**, Edinburgh (EHD-uhn-buhr-uh) Castle looms large over the city of Edinburgh, Scotland. For about 1,500 years, the stronghold on Castle Rock has offered protection and comfort for whoever called Scotland home.

As wars were waged and blood was spilled on Castle Rock, stories of **paranormal** activity grew. Many people claim that witches, ghosts, and **tortured** souls roam the stony **battlements**.

Hidden rooms and cold, dark passageways give an air of mystery to one of the oldest castles in Europe. What secrets are hidden inside its ancient walls?

THE ROCK

Edinburgh Castle sits on a crag, the rocky cliffs created by an old volcano. Icebergs carved away land, leaving the hard crag and the slope behind it. Since there's only one way to reach the top and you can see for miles around from up there, it was a perfect place to build a castle.

Over 3,000 years of history
are hidden at Castle Rock.

5

FIRST SETTLERS

Edinburgh Castle is over 900 years old, but Castle Rock has been in use for even longer. People first settled it around 900 BC.

A settlement named Din Eidyn, meaning "the stronghold of Eidyn," was established on Castle Rock around the year AD 600. It was captured by the Angles, people from the area now called Germany, in 638 and renamed Edinburgh.

Castle Rock became the home to a royal castle in the Middle Ages. In 1093, Margaret, the queen of Scotland, died in the "Castle of Maidens." Her son, King David I, built a castle around 1130. The chapel—built in honor of his mother—still stands today!

THE CHAPEL

St. Margaret's Chapel is the oldest building still standing at Edinburgh Castle. It was built in memory of Queen Margaret, who some say died of a broken heart at the castle. Starting in the 16th century, it was used to store gunpowder, but it became a place of prayer again in 1845.

Some of the buildings of Edinburgh Castle have stood for almost 1,000 years!

BACK AND FORTH

During the 13th and 14th centuries, the castle changed hands between the English and Scots many times. The **sieges** and battles took their toll on the castle walls. Under Scottish control in 1356, King David II rebuilt the castle, and it lasted until a 3-year siege in the 1570s that ended in its ruin. In 1566, Mary, Queen of Scots gave birth at Edinburgh to her son, who became King James VI of Scotland and King James I of England.

Soon after, Edinburgh Castle became a military fortress and prison rather than a place for royalty. The last member of royalty to stay there was Charles I in 1633.

This print shows Edinburgh Castle during the Lang Siege, a military action against those who held Edinburgh Castle in 1573.

570 Foot highe

The GENERALS two tents

IN THE PIT

The **dungeons** and vaults of Edinburgh Castle held prisoners who may be ghosts today! In fact, under the floorboards of King James's birth chamber is a small but very deep pit. No one knows who—or what—was put in there. There were also secret windows called "laird's lugs," or lord's ears, that let kings spy on meetings in the castle's Great Hall.

9

ESCAPE GONE WRONG

Like those found in other castles, Edinburgh's many dungeons were dark, cold cells—and some prisoners were tortured there. Horrible conditions and fears of a painful death made many prisoners take huge risks to escape.

Stories say a prisoner once tried to escape by hiding in a **wheelbarrow** full of dung! He hoped to escape down the Royal Mile, the sloping roads leading away from the castle. Instead, he was thrown to his death when the waste was emptied over the side of the castle's cliffs.

Visitors say his ghost now haunts the castle, trying to shove tourists off the battlements. Still covered in dung, you can smell him when he gets close!

MILITARY PRISON

Over 500 French prisoners were kept at the castle during the Seven Years' War (1756-1763), but its use as a prison carried well into the 19th century. The vaults beneath the castle were also used for supporters of the American Revolution. Do their tortured spirits remain?

An escape attempt ended in death for one smelly ghost.

11

THE BLACK DINNER

One of the most horrifying moments in the castle's history came in 1440. The ruling king of Scotland, James II, was just 10 years old. Two men who helped him rule decided that the 6th Earl of Douglas, age 16, and his brother, age 14, were enemies of the throne.

Invited to the castle for a banquet, the earl and his brother happily ate with the king. At the meal's end, the head of a black bull was presented to them, a sign that the chief dinner guest would be killed.

The earl and his brother were tried for treason and **beheaded** in front of the king.

DEAD MAN'S TRIAL

Punishment of criminals in Scotland was often extreme. Once, a prisoner named Francis Maubray was killed trying to escape Edinburgh Castle. Officials decided his trial had to be completed, though, so his dead body was brought back into the courtroom, where he was found guilty of treason.

King James II begged for the lives of his dinner guests —but couldn't save them.

13

THE NOR' LOCH

In 1460, King James III ordered that the flat area below the castle's cliffs be flooded to make the castle safer from attackers. This created a loch, the Scottish word for lake.

KING JAMES III OF SCOTLAND

At first, the Nor' Loch was a beautiful and peaceful place, but it later became polluted with **sewage** and other things thrown over the cliffs of the castle. The smell of methane gas and sewage became so bad that residents suffered physical effects. They began to see things that weren't there and to get sick. The loch became a well-known place for **suicides** and punishments. It was drained in 1759.

WITCH HUNT

In the 16th century, Nor' Loch was used for witch doukings, or dunkings. Women accused of **witchcraft** had their thumbs and toes tied together and were thrown into the loch on a special stool. If they drowned, they were innocent—but dead. If they lived through the douking, they were guilty and burned at the stake.

14

The loch was meant to protect the castle, but it eventually made people sick.

15

CROWN SQUARE

The main courtyard of Edinburgh Castle is Crown Square. Originally called Palace Yard, it was renamed when the Scottish crown jewels were discovered in a hiding place there in 1818. Constructed on the south-facing part of the castle in the 15th century, the square is built on top of 120 stone vaults that run underneath the castle.

This **labyrinth** of tunnels was used for many things, including torturing and holding prisoners. During the Middle Ages, when a sickness called the black plague struck, it was used to separate those who were sick. Many who caught the plague died under Crown Square.

CASTLE MAGIC

Author J. K. Rowling lived in Edinburgh while writing some of her Harry Potter books, and many people believe the castle was the inspiration for the fictional Hogwarts School of Witchcraft and Wizardry. In 2005, Edinburgh Castle was transformed into Hogwarts for a night to celebrate the book release of *Harry Potter and the Half-Blood Prince.*

There might be ghosts of plague sufferers drifting through the Edinburgh Castle vaults under Crown Square!

GREYFRIARS BOBBY

Greyfriars Bobby, a Skye terrier, belonged to a man named John Gray. An out-of-work gardener, Gray joined the Edinburgh police and used Bobby as his watchdog.

When Gray died of an illness called tuberculosis in 1858, he was buried in Greyfriars Churchyard. Every day, Bobby would stand guard over his owner's grave. For 14 years, until his death in 1872, Bobby would only leave the churchyard when a cannon called the one o'clock gun fired from the castle. Locals would then feed the dog, who went right back to the cemetery to wait for his owner, who never returned.

HAUNTED CEMETERY

Greyfriars Churchyard became a burial ground in 1562. Many famous Scots were buried there along with Greyfriars Bobby and his owner. The grounds were also used as a prison for thousands of men sent to their deaths or to slavery in Barbados. Many claim the cemetery itself is haunted and that a ghost dog roams the grounds.

A statue of Bobby stands near the churchyard in honor of the faithful dog. However, some say his story isn't true!

MUSICAL GHOSTS

The hidden tunnels of Edinburgh are the source of many stories of paranormal activity at Edinburgh Castle. While secret vaults housed prisoners, other caverns led to the town below, along the famous Royal Mile roads.

When those tunnels were first discovered, a piper was sent down into the passages to explore. People thought they could track the piper's music and help him if anything went wrong. But while the piper was underground, his music suddenly stopped! A rescue party was sent in and searched everywhere, but the piper had vanished! Some visitors claim to hear the piper's music beneath the castle, still searching for a way out.

STILL PLAYING

The lost piper may bring the ghostly sound of bagpipes to tourists, but the Edinburgh Military Tattoo brings an amazing display of music to the castle grounds each August. One of the features of the show is the lone piper, a single bagpipe player honoring the piper lost beneath the castle.

If you dare visit the haunted castle at night, you might enjoy a performance by the Edinburgh Military Tattoo!

23

The story of the headless drummer of Edinburgh Castle is one of the eeriest tales of all! Many people claim to hear the sounds of drums playing within the castle walls when they visit.

Legend says the drumming belongs to the ghost of the headless drummer, a little boy ghost that only appears on the grounds when the castle will soon be under attack. The ghost first appeared in 1650 when English statesman Oliver Cromwell attacked the castle.

No one knows who the boy is or why he haunts the castle, but sightings of him have been reported many times over the centuries.

LAST ATTACK

With each attack on the castle, the castle's defenses were improved. By the time of the Jacobite uprising in 1745, it was stronger than ever and lasted through its final official attack, when Bonnie Prince Charlie tried—and failed—to take the castle. Since then, the headless drummer has stayed in the shadows, waiting for another reason to warn the castle of danger.

Edinburgh Castle has protected many behind its high, strong walls.

25

THE EXPERIMENT

In 2001, a scientist named Dr. Richard Wiseman ran a research project at Edinburgh Castle that studied the presence of ghosts on Castle Rock. Wiseman had 240 volunteers explore the castle over the course of 10 days. They were led through parts of the castle and asked if anything unusual happened to them.

The results were shocking. People felt drops in temperature or saw shadowy figures in areas where ghosts were reported in the past. One person felt burning on their arm, while others said they felt like they were being watched.

Wiseman's results didn't prove anything, but they have definitely added to the castle's legend.

SPOOKY RESULTS

None of the volunteers knew about the hauntings at Edinburgh Castle, but they left as believers. One person saw a ghost wearing a leather apron, a ghost other tourists had reported seeing before! Another volunteer left crying after she heard loud breathing from an unoccupied corner of a room. Wiseman said the results surprised even him.

With such a grisly past, it's no wonder ghosts would haunt Edinburgh Castle's halls and walls!

CASTLE ROCK TODAY

Today, Edinburgh Castle is one of the most popular tourist attractions in Europe. Its walls are visited by over a million people a year, second in the United Kingdom only to the Tower of London. There are centuries of history to discover at Castle Rock, but with its history come strange stories and ghosts of the past.

Could you face the dungeons of Edinburgh yourself? Would you survive a walk down a dark, damp hallway deep inside the most haunted castle in Europe? Perhaps you'd like to try to find the piper lost so many years ago in the underground tunnels. The spirits of the past are waiting!

STILL ON GUARD

While Historic Scotland operates the castle for the Scottish government, Edinburgh Castle is far from a simple tourist attraction. The Scottish Division still occupies buildings on the site, while the military guards the main gate of the castle. Even in times of peace, the castle remains on guard.

The creepy stories about ghosts and witches don't keep people away from beautiful Edinburgh Castle.

29

GLOSSARY

battlement: a wall with open spaces to shoot through

behead: to remove a person's head

dungeon: a dark prison, usually underground

labyrinth: a maze

paranormal: not able to be explained by science

sewage: waste, usually human

siege: the use of military to surround an area or building in order to capture it

suicide: the act of killing oneself

tortured: in a state of suffering great pain of the body or mind, or to cause such suffering

volcano: an opening in a planet's surface through which hot, liquid rock sometimes flows

wheelbarrow: a small cart with two handles and one wheel

witchcraft: the use of sorcery or magic

FOR MORE INFORMATION

BOOKS

Belanger, Jeff. *World's Most Haunted Places*. New York, NY: Rosen Publishing, 2009.

Knox, Barbara. *Edinburgh Castle: Scotland's Haunted Fortress*. New York, NY: Bearport Publishing, 2007.

WEBSITES

Edinburgh Castle

www.edinburghcastle.gov.uk
Discover more about Castle Rock and plan a tour of Edinburgh Castle.

Edinburgh Castle

www.edinburgh-royalmile.com/castle/edinburgh_castle.html
Learn more about the areas surrounding Castle Rock.

INDEX

black plague 16, 17

Castle Rock 4, 5, 6, 18, 26, 28

cemetery 20

Crown Square 16, 17

David I, King 6

David II, King 8

Din Eidyn 6

Douglas, Janet 18

doukings 14, 18

dungeons 9, 10, 28

Edinburgh 4, 6, 17, 22, 28

fortress 8

ghosts 4, 9, 10, 11, 17, 20, 24,
      26, 27, 28, 29

Great Hall 9

Greyfriars Bobby 20, 21

Greyfriars Churchyard 20, 21

headless drummer 24

James II, King 12, 13

James III, King 14

James VI, King 8, 9

Margaret, Queen 6

Mary, Queen of Scots 8

Nor' Loch 14, 15

piper 22, 28

prison 8, 10, 20

prisoners 9, 10, 12, 16, 18, 22

research project 26

Rowling, J. K. 17

Scotland 4, 6, 8, 18

St. Margaret's Chapel 6

tunnels 16, 17, 22, 28

volcano 4

Wiseman, Richard 26

witches 4, 14, 18, 19, 29

Witches' Well 18, 19